Party games

Text written by Alison Hawes
Illustrated by Mirella Mariani

How to help your child read this book

This book gives your child extra practice in reading a story that includes sounds
he or she has learnt at school.

Ask your child to read the Story Green Words and Red Words below, before reading the
story. Do not read the story to your child first. Point to the words as he or she reads.
If your child hesitates, help him or her to sound-blend the word.

Re-read each sentence or page to keep the plot moving. Children's attention is focused
on reading the words and they find it hard to focus on the story at the same time.

Don't make them struggle too much and praise them when they succeed.
Do it all with patience and love!

Story Green Words

Story Green Words are made up of sounds your child has already learnt.
This book contains the following green words:

labels   mittens   chopsticks   space   ankles

make   garden   buckets   dice

Red Words

Red Words are harder to read because the letters represent unusual sounds.
Ask your child to read the red words, but if he or she gets stuck on a word,
read the word to your child. This book contains the following red words:

your   other   are   they   two   some

put   ball   do   water

Important note

Read stories to your children that are beyond the level they can read for themselves – every evening. They'll only want to become readers if they experience the joy of listening to a range of stories, non-fiction and poetry. Very soon, they will be able to read those books for themselves, as well as listen to them.

Vocabulary check

Tell your child the meaning of each word in the context of the story.

	definition:	sentence:
mittens	gloves without fingers	Put on the mittens ...
chopsticks	sticks used to pick up food	... grab the chopsticks and pick up the chocolates.
ankle	the part that connects your foot to your leg	... fix them to your ankles with the string.
stomp	put your foot on something	Stomp on the other balloons to make them pop!

The Name Game

This is a good game to get a party started.

To play this game

1. You will need sticky labels with animal names on them.
2. Ask an adult to stick an animal's name on your face!
3. Quiz the other boys and girls about which animal you are. They can say yes or no.

7

The Chocolate Game

This is a game that boys and girls enjoy playing!

To play this game

1. You will need some chocolates, a pair of mittens, a pair of chopsticks, and a dice.
2. Place the chocolates, mittens and chopsticks in the middle of the group.
3. When you throw a six, it is your go.

4. Put on the mittens, grab the chopsticks and pick up the chocolates – if you can!

The Balloon Stomp Game

You will need a lot of space to play this game.
It can get very loud!

To play this game

1. You will need a big packet of balloons and a ball of string.
2. Blow up two balloons and fix them to your ankles with the string. Ask the other boys and girls to do the same.

3. Stomp on the other balloons to make them pop!
4. The last boy or girl left with a balloon wins.

The Water Race

This messy game is best played in the garden.

To play this game

1. Get into groups.
2. A group will need a cup and two buckets (a bucket at the start and a bucket at the finish).
3. Fill the bucket at the start with water.
4. When it is your go to race, fill the cup with water from the first bucket. Then race to the second bucket and tip the water in.
5. At the end of the race, the group with more water in the second bucket wins.

Questions to read and answer

Ask your child to read the sentences and choose the correct answer.

1. The **Name / Chocolate / Balloon Stomp** Game is a good game to get a party started.

2. You must throw a **three / six / ten** to have a go at The Chocolate Game.

3. The Balloon Stomp Game can get very **messy / loud / wet**.

4. The Water Race is best played in the **house / bedroom / garden**.

Explain the text

Take turns explaining the text with your child.